The Baker's Appendix

The Baker's Appendix

THE ESSENTIAL KITCHEN COMPANION

with Deliciously Dependable, Infinitely Adaptable Recipes

Jessica Reed

CLARKSON POTTER/PUBLISHERS

New York

All rights reserved.
Published in the United States by Clarkson Potter/
Publishers, an imprint of the Crown Publishing
Group, a division of Penguin Random House LLC,
New York.
crownpublishing.com
clarksonpotter.com

CLARKSON POTTER is a trademark and
POTTER with colophon is a registered trademark
of Penguin Random House LLC.

Originally self-published by the author
in different form in 2014.

Library of Congress Cataloging-in-Publication Data
Names: Reed, Jessica, 1976– author.
Title: The baker's appendix / Jessica Reed.
Description: First edition. | New York : Clarkson
Potter [2017] | Includes index.
Identifiers: LCCN 2016016512 | ISBN 9780451495747
(hardcover : alk. paper) | ISBN 9780451495754
(ebook)
Subjects: LCSH: Baking—Handbooks, manuals, etc.
Classification: LCC TX763 2017 | DDC 641.81/
5—dc23 LC record available at
https://lccn.loc.gov/2016016512

ISBN 978-0-451-49574-7
Ebook ISBN 978-0-451-49575-4

Printed in China

Book design by Marysarah Quinn
Illustrations by Pop Chart Lab
Cover design by Marysarah Quinn

10 9 8 7 6 5 4 3 2 1

First Edition

CONTENTS

INTRODUCTION

I fell in love with baking over a decade ago, tinkering in my tiny kitchen with tools purchased from a nearby dollar store and a stack of beautiful, albeit unwieldy, baking books. While these volumes worked well propped open to a particular recipe, when I needed to figure out a conversion or substitution on the fly, mess tended to ensue. Maybe it's just me, but maneuvering the massive book (or books, as I was never able to find what I needed in just one appendix) and flipping pages back and forth among bowls filled with flour and sugar and measuring cups holding gelatinous eggs and slick oil almost always led to disaster. Add to the mix a smartphone or computer, and the chances for trouble only intensified.

Desiring a more convenient (and cleaner!) solution, I began collecting notes, photocopies, and printouts in a file folder kept wedged between half-sheet pans on a kitchen shelf. That worked just fine for some time, but when I discovered the joy of using a kitchen scale (precision is wonderful, but fewer dishes more so!), I started cramming many more pages filled with notes on common baking ingredients and their weights into the folder—and it became just as inconvenient as all of those books.

Those haphazardly collected and butter-smeared pages, as well as my mistakes and triumphs in the kitchen, are what led to *The Baker's Appendix*. I figured if I was so in need of such a resource, maybe other bakers would be as well. A helpful tool for the home baker, it is intended to be compact enough that you can keep it wedged between baking pans or tucked into a drawer—a quick, easy-to-navigate reference book that you can count on both before and during the baking process. And, well, I wanted it to be delightful to look at too, so that you'll love having it constantly on hand.

The information contained herein has been gleaned from a variety of print and online resources, as well as my own compiled calculations and measurements made using a My Weight Baker's Math Kitchen Scale, professional-grade stainless-steel dry measuring cups and spoons, and a 1-quart Pyrex liquid measuring cup.

Please note that the gram counts in the Common Ingredients in Cups and Grams section (page 24) are not law but rather rules of thumb for home bakers; many factors can affect the weight of your ingredients by gram increments (flours are especially variable). Temperature, time of year, age of ingredient, manufacturer, and the method of measurement all play a role. Additionally, some minimal liberties were taken; if similar ingredients weighed within a few grams of each other, I grouped them together for ease of reference and remembering. The same reasoning applies to why I have used only grams and not milliliter measurement for liquids; on the lower end, gram and milliliter measurements are comparable.

Beyond providing numbers, formulas, and substitutions that can help make baking easier, I've also included simple how-tos (page 93), decorating tips (page 101), a selection of dependable recipes (page 54), and more. I'm especially proud of the recipes, which really are foolproof. You won't find anything too unusual or complicated, but rather classic cakes, cookies, quick breads/muffins, frostings, and fillings that are not only simple, but open to endless mixing, matching, and experimentation. I've given nine variations with the quick bread recipe alone! And those are just the tip of the iceberg.

I hope that *The Baker's Appendix* is a great companion for you in your kitchen endeavors, whether you're a professional pastry chef with decades of experience and the ability to make macarons in your sleep (I'll get there one day!) or someone new to the beauty of baking, to the way a cake or a loaf of bread or a pie can bring such joy to yourself and all of those around you. It is one of life's simplest pleasures. May this book make the experience all the simpler.

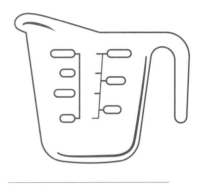

CONVERSIONS

Adjusting for Altitude

	3,000 ft	5,000 ft	7,000 ft	10,000 ft
Flour	increase each cup by 1 tbsp	increase each cup by 2 tbsp	increase each cup by 3 tbsp	increase each cup by 4 tbsp
Baking Powder or Soda	decrease each tsp by ⅛	decrease each tsp by ¼	decrease each tsp by ½	decrease each tsp by ⅔
Sugar	decrease each cup by 1 tbsp	decrease each cup by 2 tbsp	decrease each cup by 3 tbsp	decrease each cup by 4 tbsp
Liquid	increase each cup by 1 tbsp	increase each cup by 2 tbsp	increase each cup by 3 tbsp	increase each cup by 4 tbsp

Oven Temperature Conversions

NOTE: I can not stress highly enough how important an oven thermometer is for baking. If you don't have one, buy one. CDN makes reliable models.

OVEN MARK	FAHRENHEIT	CELSIUS	GAS
Very Slow/Cool	250°–275°F	130°–140°C	Gas Mark ½–1
Slow/Cool	300°F	150°C	Gas Mark 2
Moderately Slow/Warm	325°F	170°C	Gas Mark 3
Moderate	350°F	180°C	Gas Mark 4
Moderately Hot	375°–400°F	190°–200°C	Gas Mark 5–6
Hot	425°–450°F	220°–230°C	Gas Mark 7–8
Very Hot	450°–475°F	230°–250°C	Gas Mark 8–9
Extremely Hot	475°–500°F	250°–260°C	Gas Mark 9–10

Using a convection oven instead of a standard oven

I've not had the opportunity to bake using a convection oven, but since they are becoming more and more common, I wanted to include guidelines for doing so. There is no direct conversion, but there are two generally accepted methods:

1. Reduce the temperature by 25°F/15°C.
2. Reduce the baking time by 25%.

Baking Pan Volume Conversions

If your recipe calls for a particular pan that you either don't have or
do not care to use, look in this section for a pan (or pans) that will
hold an equal or greater volume. Remember to adjust baking time
accordingly: for a smaller pan, increase the baking time; for a larger
pan, decrease the baking time.

ROUND

DIMENSIONS	VOLUME
6" × 2" (15 cm x 5 cm)	4 c (950 mL)
8" × 2" (20 cm × 5 cm)	6 c (1.4 L)
8" × 3" (20 cm × 8 cm)	7 c (1.6 L)
9" × 2" (23 cm × 5 cm)	8 c (1.9 L)
9" × 3" (23 cm × 8 cm)	8¾ c (2 L)
10" × 2" (25 cm × 5 cm)	11 c (2.6 L)

SQUARE

DIMENSIONS	VOLUME
6" × 6" × 2" (15 cm × 15 cm × 5 cm)	6 c (1.4 L)
8" × 8" × 2" (20 cm × 20 cm × 5 cm)	8 c (1.9 L)
9" × 9" × 2" (23 cm × 23 cm × 5 cm)	10 c (2.4 L)

RECTANGULAR

DIMENSIONS	VOLUME
7" × 11" × 2" (18 cm × 28 cm × 5 cm)	6 c (1.4 L)
9" × 13" × 2" (23 cm × 33 cm × 5 cm)	14 c (3.3 L)

BUNDT

DIMENSIONS	VOLUME
7.5" × 3" (19 cm × 8 cm)	6 c (1.4 L)
10" × 3.5" (25 cm × 9 cm)	12 c (2.8 L)

TUBE

DIMENSIONS	VOLUME
8" × 3" (20 cm × 8 cm)	9 c (2.1 L)
9" × 3" (23 cm × 8 cm)	12 c (2.8 L)
10" × 4" (25 cm × 10 cm)	16 c (3.8 L)

LOAF

DIMENSIONS	VOLUME
8" × 4" × 2.5" (20 cm × 10 cm × 6 cm)	4 c (950 mL)
8.5" × 4.5" × 2.5" (21 cm × 11 cm × 6 cm)	6 c (1.4 L)
9" × 5" × 3" (23 cm × 13 cm × 8 cm)	8 c (1.9 L)

JELLY ROLL/SHEET PAN

DIMENSIONS	VOLUME
9" × 12.5" × 1" (23 cm × 32 cm × 2.5 cm)	6 c (1.4 L)
10.5" × 15.5" × 1" (27 cm × 39 cm × 2.5 cm)	10 c (2.4 L)
12.5" × 17.5" × 1" (32 cm × 44 cm × 2.5 cm)	12 c (2.8 L)

PIE

DIMENSIONS	VOLUME
9" × 1.5" (23 cm × 4 cm)	4 c (950 mL)
9.5" × 2" (24 cm × 5 cm)	7 c (1.6 L)

TART

DIMENSIONS	VOLUME
4" × 0.75" (10 cm × 2 cm)	½ c (120 mL)
9" × 1" (23 cm × 2.5 cm)	4 c (950 mL)

CUPCAKE/MUFFIN TIN

	DIMENSIONS	VOLUME
MINI	1.5" × 0.75" (3.5 cm × 2 cm)	⅛ c (30 mL)
STANDARD	2.5" × 1.5" (6 cm × 3.5 cm)	¼ c (60 mL)
JUMBO	3.5" × 2" (7 cm × 5 cm)	½ c (120 mL)

SPRINGFORM

DIMENSIONS	VOLUME
6" × 3" (15 cm × 8 cm)	4 c (950 mL)
8" × 3" (20 cm × 8 cm)	10 c (2.4 L)
9" × 3" (23 cm × 8 cm)	11 c (2.6 L)
10" × 3" (25 cm × 8 cm)	12 c (2.8 L)

Fraction to Decimal

FRACTION	DECIMAL	FRACTION	DECIMAL
$\frac{1}{64}$	0.015625	$\frac{9}{32}$	0.28125
$\frac{1}{32}$	0.03125	$\frac{19}{64}$	0.296875
$\frac{3}{64}$	0.046875	$\frac{5}{16}$	0.3125
$\frac{1}{16}$	0.0625	$\frac{21}{64}$	0.328125
$\frac{5}{64}$	0.078125	$\frac{11}{32}$	0.34375
$\frac{3}{32}$	0.09375	$\frac{23}{64}$	0.359375
$\frac{7}{64}$	0.109375	$\frac{3}{8}$	0.375
$\frac{1}{8}$	0.125	$\frac{25}{64}$	0.390625
$\frac{9}{64}$	0.140625	$\frac{13}{32}$	0.40625
$\frac{5}{32}$	0.15625	$\frac{27}{64}$	0.421875
$\frac{11}{64}$	0.171875	$\frac{7}{16}$	0.4375
$\frac{3}{16}$	0.1875	$\frac{29}{64}$	0.453125
$\frac{13}{64}$	0.203125	$\frac{15}{32}$	0.46875
$\frac{7}{32}$	0.21875	$\frac{31}{64}$	0.484375
$\frac{15}{64}$	0.234375	$\frac{1}{2}$	0.50
$\frac{1}{4}$	0.25	$\frac{33}{64}$	0.515625
$\frac{17}{64}$	0.265625	$\frac{17}{32}$	0.53125

FRACTION	DECIMAL	FRACTION	DECIMAL
$^{35}/_{64}$	0.546875	$^{25}/_{32}$	0.78125
$^{9}/_{16}$	0.5625	$^{51}/_{64}$	0.796875
$^{37}/_{64}$	0.578125	$^{13}/_{16}$	0.8125
$^{19}/_{32}$	0.59375	$^{53}/_{64}$	0.828125
$^{39}/_{64}$	0.609375	$^{27}/_{32}$	0.84375
$^{5}/_{8}$	0.625	$^{55}/_{64}$	0.859375
$^{41}/_{64}$	0.640625	$^{7}/_{8}$	0.875
$^{21}/_{32}$	0.65625	$^{57}/_{64}$	0.890625
$^{43}/_{64}$	0.67185	$^{29}/_{32}$	0.90625
$^{11}/_{16}$	0.6875	$^{59}/_{64}$	0.921875
$^{45}/_{64}$	0.703125	$^{15}/_{16}$	0.9375
$^{23}/_{32}$	0.71875	$^{61}/_{64}$	0.953125
$^{47}/_{64}$	0.734375	$^{31}/_{32}$	0.96875
$^{3}/_{4}$	0.75	$^{63}/_{64}$	0.984375
$^{49}/_{64}$	0.765625	1	1.00

Historical Measurement Conversions

60 drops = 1 tsp

Butter the size of a walnut = 2 tbsp

Butter the size of an egg = ¼ c

Coffee cup = 1 c

Dash = ⅛ tsp

Dessert spoon = 1½ tsp

Gill = ½ c

Handful = ½ c

Pinch = ⅛ tsp

Salt spoon = ¼ tsp

Teacup = ½ c

Tin cup = 1 c

Tumbler full = 2 c

Wineglass = ¼ c

Sugar Syrup Temperatures

NOTE: The temperatures given are for sea level.
For every 1,000 feet above sea level, subtract 2°F (1°C).

215°–234°F: THREAD

234°–240°F: SOFT BALL

242°–248°F: FIRM BALL

250°–268°F: HARD BALL

270°–290°F: SOFT CRACK

300°–310°F: HARD CRACK

320°–350°F: CARAMEL

Volume Conversions

1 c	16 tbsp
2 c	1 pint
1 pint	16 fl oz
4 c	1 quart
1 quart	32 fl oz
8 pints	4 quarts
4 quarts	1 gallon
1 L	34 fl oz
1 gallon	3.75 L

CUP	FLUID OZ	TBSP	TSP	ML
			¼ tsp	1 mL
			½ tsp	2 mL
			1 tsp	5 mL
		½ tbsp	1.5 tsp	7 mL
		1 tbsp	3 tsp	15 mL
⅛ c	1 fl oz	2 tbsp	6 tsp	30 mL
¼ c	2 fl oz	4 tbsp	12 tsp	60 mL
⅓ c	2.5 fl oz	5 tbsp	15 tsp	75 mL
½ c	4 fl oz	8 tbsp	24 tsp	125 mL
⅔ c	5 fl oz	10 tbsp	30 tsp	150 mL
¾ c	6 fl oz	12 tbsp		175 mL
1 c	8 fl oz	16 tbsp		250 mL
1¼ c	10 fl oz			300 mL
1½ c	12 fl oz			350 mL
2 c	16 fl oz			500 mL

Unusual Measurement Conversions

A pinch	⅛ tsp
A dash	a few drops
½ tsp	30 drops
A dram	¾ tsp
1 jigger	3 tbsp
⅓ cup	5 tbsp + 1 tsp
⅜ cup	¼ cup + 2 tbsp
⅔ cup	10 tbsp + 2 tsp
⅝ cup	½ cup + 2 tbsp
⅞ cup	¾ cup + 2 tbsp

Weight Conversions

OUNCES	GRAMS	OUNCES	GRAMS
¼ oz	7 g	8 oz	225 g
½ oz	15 g	9 oz	250 g
1 oz	30 g	10 oz	300 g
2 oz	55 g	11 oz	325 g
3 oz	86 g	12 oz	340 g
4 oz	115 g	13 oz	375 g
5 oz	150 g	14 oz	400 g
6 oz	175 g	15 oz	425 g
7 oz	200 g	16 oz (1 lb)	455 g

1 oz = approximately 28.35 g

Common Ingredients in Cups and Grams

CHOCOLATE

Chocolate Chips/Shavings

CUPS	GRAMS
1	170
¾	128
⅔	113
½	85
⅓	57
¼	43
⅛	21
1 tbsp	11
1 tsp	4

Cocoa Nibs

CUPS	GRAMS
1	120
¾	90
⅔	80
½	60
⅓	40
¼	30
⅛	15
1 tbsp	8
1 tsp	3

Cocoa Powder

CUPS	GRAMS
1	85
¾	64
⅔	50
½	43
⅓	25
¼	21
⅛	10
1 tbsp	5
1 tsp	2

DAIRY AND NONDAIRY

Cottage Cheese
Cream Cheese
Ricotta Cheese

Milk • Buttermilk
Sour Cream • Heavy Cream
Yogurt • Crème Fraîche
Almond Milk • Soy Milk
Oat Milk • Rice Milk
Coconut Milk

CUPS	GRAMS
1	225
¾	169
⅔	150
½	112
⅓	75
¼	56
⅛	28
1 tbsp	14
1 tsp	5

CUPS	GRAMS
1	240
¾	180
⅔	160
½	120
⅓	80
¼	60
⅛	30
1 tbsp	15
1 tsp	5

EGGS

NOTE: The weights given constitute the average for eggs of that size.

> MEDIUM IN SHELL: 1.75 oz/51 g
> MEDIUM OUT OF SHELL: 1.65 oz/47 g
> MEDIUM WHITE: 1 oz/30 g
> MEDIUM YOLK: 0.6 oz/17 g
>
> LARGE IN SHELL: 2 oz/56 g
> LARGE OUT OF SHELL: 1.75 oz/50 g
> LARGE WHITE: 1.05 oz/30 g
> LARGE YOLK: 0.65 oz/18.6 g
>
> EXTRA-LARGE IN SHELL: 2.25 oz/66 g
> EXTRA-LARGE OUT OF SHELL: 1.8 oz/52 g
> EXTRA-LARGE WHITE: 1.1 oz/31 g
> EXTRA-LARGE YOLK: 0.7 oz/21 g
>
> JUMBO IN SHELL: 2.5 oz/73g
> JUMBO OUT OF SHELL: 2.1 oz/60 g
> JUMBO WHITE: 1.35 oz/38 g
> JUMBO YOLK: 0.75 oz/22 g

FATS

Oil

Butter • Margarine
Lard • Shortening

CUPS	GRAMS
1	224
¾	168
⅔	149
½	112
⅓	75
¼	56
⅛	28
1 tbsp	14
1 tsp	5

CUPS	GRAMS
1	227*
¾	170
⅔	150
½	113†
⅓	76
¼	57
⅛	28
1 tbsp	14
1 tsp	5

*2 standard (4 oz.) American sticks
†1 standard (4 oz.) American stick

FLOURS

All-Purpose

CUPS	GRAMS
1	125
¾	94
⅔	83
½	63
⅓	42
¼	31
⅛	15
1 tbsp	8
1 tsp	3

Bread

CUPS	GRAMS
1	127
¾	95
⅔	85
½	64
⅓	42
¼	32
⅛	16
1 tbsp	8
1 tsp	3

continues

FLOURS *continued*

Buckwheat

CUPS	GRAMS
1	120
¾	90
⅔	80
½	60
⅓	40
¼	30
⅛	15
1 tbsp	8
1 tsp	3

Cake

CUPS	GRAMS
1	100
¾	75
⅔	67
½	50
⅓	33
¼	25
⅛	13
1 tbsp	6
1 tsp	2

Chestnut

CUPS	GRAMS
1	100
¾	75
⅔	67
½	50
⅓	33
¼	25
⅛	13
1 tbsp	6
1 tsp	2

Coconut

CUPS	GRAMS
1	120
¾	90
⅔	80
½	60
⅓	40
¼	30
⅛	15
1 tbsp	5
1 tsp	2

continues

FLOURS *continued*

Cornmeal

CUPS	GRAMS
1	150
¾	113
⅔	100
½	75
⅓	50
¼	38
⅛	19
1 tbsp	9
1 tsp	3

Gluten-Free Commercial Blends
(Cup4Cup and Bob's Red Mill)

CUPS	GRAMS
1	136
¾	102
⅔	91
½	68
⅓	45
¼	34
⅛	17
1 tbsp	9
1 tsp	3

Graham

Nut Meals (Almond, Hazelnut, Pecan, Pistachio, Walnut, etc.)

CUPS	GRAMS
1	120
¾	90
⅔	80
½	60
⅓	40
¼	30
⅛	15
1 tbsp	5
1 tsp	2

CUPS	GRAMS
1	96
¾	72
⅔	64
½	48
⅓	32
¼	24
⅛	12
1 tbsp	6
1 tsp	2

continues

FLOURS *continued*

Oat

CUPS	GRAMS
1	90
¾	68
⅔	60
½	45
⅓	30
¼	23
⅛	11
1 tbsp	6
1 tsp	2

Pastry

CUPS	GRAMS
1	100
¾	81
⅔	72
½	54
⅓	36
¼	27
⅛	14
1 tbsp	7
1 tsp	2

Rice (White and Brown)

CUPS	GRAMS
1	150
¾	113
⅔	100
½	75
⅓	50
¼	38
⅛	19
1 tbsp	9
1 tsp	3

Rye

CUPS	GRAMS
1	102
¾	77
⅔	68
½	51
⅓	34
¼	26
⅛	13
1 tbsp	6
1 tsp	2

continues

FLOURS *continued*

Sorghum

CUPS	GRAMS
1	120
¾	90
⅔	80
½	60
⅓	40
¼	30
⅛	15
1 tbsp	8
1 tsp	3

Spelt

CUPS	GRAMS
1	120
¾	90
⅔	80
½	60
⅓	40
¼	30
⅛	15
1 tbsp	8
1 tsp	3

Teff

CUPS	GRAMS
1	130
¾	98
⅔	87
½	65
⅓	43
¼	33
⅛	16
1 tbsp	8
1 tsp	3

Whole-Wheat

CUPS	GRAMS
1	130
¾	98
⅔	87
½	65
⅓	43
¼	33
⅛	16
1 tbsp	8
1 tsp	3

continues

FLOURS *continued*

Whole-Wheat Pastry

CUPS	GRAMS
1	120
¾	90
⅔	80
½	60
⅓	40
¼	30
⅛	15
1 tbsp	8
1 tsp	3

LEAVENERS AND THICKENERS

Baking Powder

	GRAMS
1 tbsp	15
1 tsp	5

Gelatin, Powdered

	GRAMS
1 tbsp	12
1 tsp	4

Baking Soda

	GRAMS
1 tbsp	15
1 tsp	5

*Yeast, Active Dry**

	GRAMS
1 tbsp	9
1 tsp	3

One packet = ¼ oz = 2¼ tsp = 7 g

Cornstarch

	GRAMS
1 tbsp	8
1 tsp	3

Yeast, Instant

	GRAMS
1 tbsp	6
1 tsp	2

NUTS

Nuts, Whole/Unshelled

CUPS	GRAMS
1	142
¾	106
⅔	79
½	71
⅓	45
¼	36
⅛	18
1 tbsp	9
1 tsp	3

Nuts, Chopped/Slivered

CUPS	GRAMS
1	113
¾	85
⅔	75
½	57
⅓	38
¼	28
⅛	14
1 tbsp	7
1 tsp	2

Nut Butters
(Peanut, Almond, Cashew, etc.)

CUPS	GRAMS
1	256
¾	192
⅔	170
½	128
⅓	85
¼	64
⅛	32
1 tbsp	16
1 tsp	5

SPICES, EXTRACTS, AND FLAVORINGS

Salt, Kosher

	GRAMS
1 tbsp	9
1 tsp	3

Finely Ground Spices

	GRAMS
1 tbsp	6
1 tsp	2

Salt, Table

	GRAMS
1 tbsp	18
1 tsp	6

Liquid Extracts

	GRAMS
1 tbsp	13
1 tsp	4

SWEETENERS

Agave Nectar • Brown Rice Syrup
Corn Syrup • Honey
Maple Syrup • Molasses

Brown Sugar or
Muscovado, Packed

CUPS	GRAMS
1	336
¾	255
⅔	226
½	170
⅓	113
¼	85
⅛	42
1 tbsp	21
1 tsp	7

CUPS	GRAMS
1	220
¾	165
⅔	147
½	110
⅓	73
¼	55
⅛	28
1 tbsp	14
1 tsp	5

continues

SWEETENERS *continued*

Coconut Sugar

CUPS	GRAMS
1	150
¾	114
⅔	100
½	75
⅓	50
¼	38
⅛	19
1 tbsp	10
1 tsp	3

Confectioners' Sugar

CUPS	GRAMS
1	120
¾	90
⅔	80
½	60
⅓	40
¼	30
⅛	15
1 tbsp	7
1 tsp	2

Granulated (Standard White),
Castor, and Turbinado

CUPS	GRAMS
1	200
¾	150
⅔	133
½	100
⅓	67
¼	50
⅛	25
1 tbsp	12
1 tsp	4

Sugar Substitutes
(Splenda for Baking
and Truvia Baking Blend)

CUPS	GRAMS
1	200
¾	150
⅔	133
½	100
⅓	67
¼	50
⅛	25
1 tbsp	12
1 tsp	4

VARIOUS MIX-INS

Almond Paste/Marzipan

CUPS	GRAMS
1	260
¾	195
⅔	173
½	130
⅓	87
¼	65
⅛	33
1 tbsp	16
1 tsp	5

Applesauce

CUPS	GRAMS
1	240
¾	180
⅔	160
½	120
⅓	80
¼	60
⅛	30
1 tbsp	15
1 tsp	5

Banana, Mashed

CUPS	GRAMS
1	227
¾	171
⅔	151
½	114
⅓	76
¼	57
⅛	28
1 tbsp	14
1 tsp	5

Carrots, Grated

CUPS	GRAMS
1	99
¾	74
⅔	66
½	48
⅓	33
¼	25
⅛	12
1 tbsp	6
1 tsp	2

continues

VARIOUS MIX-INS *continued*

Chia Seeds (for all other seeds, see Seeds, Whole)

CUPS	GRAMS
1	192
¾	144
⅔	128
½	96
⅓	64
¼	48
⅛	24
1 tbsp	12
1 tsp	4

Coconut (Dried, Shredded, or Flaked)

CUPS	GRAMS
1	50
¾	38
⅔	33
½	25
⅓	17
¼	13
⅛	7
1 tbsp	3
1 tsp	1

Dried Fruit, Small Pieces/Dice

CUPS	GRAMS
1	128
¾	96
⅔	85
½	64
⅓	43
¼	32
⅛	16
1 tbsp	8
1 tsp	3

Flax Meal

CUPS	GRAMS
1	104
¾	78
⅔	70
½	52
⅓	35
¼	26
⅛	13
1 tbsp	6
1 tsp	2

continues

VARIOUS MIX-INS *continued*

Graham Cracker Crumbs

CUPS	GRAMS
1	130*
¾	98
⅔	87
½	65
⅓	42
¼	33
⅛	16
1 tbsp	8
1 tsp	3

*One sleeve of commercial boxed
graham crackers = 9 crackers =
1 c = 130 g crumbs

Jam, Jelly, and Preserves

CUPS	GRAMS
1	320
¾	240
⅔	213
½	160
⅓	107
¼	80
⅛	40
1 tbsp	20
1 tsp	7

Mayonnaise

CUPS	GRAMS
1	224
¾	168
⅔	149
½	112
⅓	75
¼	56
⅛	28
1 tbsp	14
1 tsp	4

Oats, Traditional Rolled

CUPS	GRAMS
1	80
¾	60
⅔	53
½	40
⅓	27
¼	20
⅛	10
1 tbsp	5
1 tsp	2

continues

VARIOUS MIX-INS *continued*

Pineapple, Crushed or Chunks, Drained

CUPS	GRAMS
1	200
¾	150
⅔	133
½	100
⅓	67
¼	50
⅛	25
1 tbsp	13
1 tsp	4

Pumpkin Puree, Canned

CUPS	GRAMS
1	244
¾	183
⅔	162
½	122
⅓	81
¼	61
⅛	31
1 tbsp	16
1 tsp	5

Seeds, Whole (Flax, Poppy,
Sunflower, Sesame, etc.)

CUPS	GRAMS
1	142
¾	107
⅔	95
½	71
⅓	47
¼	36
⅛	18
1 tbsp	9
1 tsp	3

Wheat Bran
and Wheat Germ

CUPS	GRAMS
1	60
¾	45
⅔	40
½	30
⅓	20
¼	15
⅛	8
1 tbsp	4
1 tsp	1

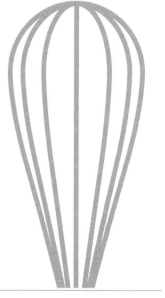

RECIPES

CAKES, COOKIES, QUICK BREADS, AND MUFFINS

The recipes in this section were developed to be simple, dependable, classic, and adaptable. These are the kinds of recipes that you can whip up at a moment's(ish) notice—cakes and cookies that come together quickly and can be baked right away, with nary a need to fold in egg whites.

NOTE: All recipes may be made gluten-free by substituting equal amounts of Cup4Cup gluten-free flour mix for the regular flour. Also, all may be made vegan by replacing the eggs with a flax egg or other substitute, margarine or shortening, and nondairy milks.

Chocolate Cake

Makes three 8-inch (20 cm) layers, two 9-inch (23 cm) layers,
18 cupcakes, one 9 x 13-inch (23 cm x 33 cm) sheet cake,
or one 10-to-12-cup (2.4–2.8 L) Bundt cake

I have played around with *a lot* of chocolate cake recipes, and after
years of tinkering, I have finally found *the* one. Incredibly versatile,
this bakes into a not-too-sweet, very chocolaty cake that's perfect with
or without frosting. It's also super quick and easy to make and can be
mixed up with just two bowls—no stand or hand mixer required. The
espresso powder is an optional ingredient. In small amounts, coffee has
a magical power to increase the flavor of chocolate. I recommend it, but
the cake will be delicious regardless.

2 cups (250 grams) all-purpose
   flour
¾ cup (64 grams) cocoa powder
   (preferably Dutch-processed,
   but any cocoa you have is fine)
2 teaspoons baking soda
1 teaspoon kosher salt
2 teaspoons espresso powder
   (optional)

1 cup (240 grams) sour cream,
   room temperature
2 teaspoons vanilla extract
½ cup (112 grams) neutral oil, such
   as canola
1½ cups (330 grams) light or dark
   brown sugar, packed
½ cup (100 grams) granulated sugar
2 large eggs, room temperature
1 cup (240 grams) boiling water

Preheat the oven to 350°F (180°C). Prepare your pan(s) with Cake
Pan Primer (see page 96) and, depending on the pan(s), line with
parchment or cupcake papers.

In a medium bowl, sift or thoroughly whisk together the flour,
cocoa powder, baking soda, salt, and espresso powder (if using).

In a separate large bowl, whisk together the sour cream,
vanilla, oil, brown sugar, granulated sugar, and eggs until very
well combined. Gently whisk the dry ingredients into the wet
ingredients until incorporated; don't worry about any lumps or
streaks of dry ingredients at this point. Whisk in the boiling water,

¼ cup at a time, until all of the water is incorporated and you have a nice, smooth batter. (Note that this is a thin batter—maybe thinner than you are used to.) Divide the batter evenly between the prepared pan(s).

Bake for the amount of time appropriate for your pan(s) (directions follow) until the top springs back lightly when pressed, the cake starts pulling away from the side of the pan, and a toothpick inserted in the center comes out with just a few crumbs. Transfer to a wire rack and let cool for 10 minutes. Remove from the pan(s), set on wire racks, and let cool completely.

VARIATIONS

Black Chocolate: Use ½ cup (43 grams) standard cocoa powder and ¼ cup (21 grams) black cocoa powder (I get mine from kingarthurflour.com). The chocolate flavor will be deeper, and the color will be very dark.

Mint: Substitute 2 teaspoons pure mint extract for the vanilla extract and/or brush the cooled layers with Mint Cake Soak (page 90).

Orange: Rub the zest of one orange into the sugar before adding it to the wet ingredients and/or brush the cooled layers with Lemon or Orange Cake Soak (page 91) or an orange Liquor or Spirit Cake Soak (page 90).

Mexican Spice: Add 2 teaspoons ground cinnamon and ¼ teaspoon cayenne pepper to the other dry ingredients when you sift them together.

Bourbon: Brush the cooled layers with Bourbon Cake Soak (page 90).

Peanut Butter: Liberally frost with Peanut Butter Cream Cheese Frosting (page 78).

Salted Caramel: Spread Salted Caramel Sauce (page 81) over each layer; sprinkle coarse sea salt on top of the frosted cake.

20 TO 25 MINUTES FOR THREE 8-INCH (20 CM) LAYERS

25 TO 30 MINUTES FOR TWO 9-INCH (23 CM) LAYERS

16 TO 18 MINUTES FOR CUPCAKES

25 TO 30 MINUTES FOR A 9 X 13-INCH (23 CM X 33 CM) SHEET CAKE

45 TO 55 MINUTES FOR A BUNDT CAKE

1-2-3-4 Vanilla Cake

Makes three 8-inch (20 cm) layers, two 9-inch (23 cm) layers,
18 cupcakes, one 9 x 13-inch (23 cm x 33 cm) sheet cake,
or one 10-to-12-cup (2.4–2.8 L) Bundt cake

This is an adaptation of a recipe popular before standard measurements
came into play, the 1-2-3-4 referring to the basic ingredients used:
1 cup butter, 2 cups sugar, 3 cups flour, and 4 eggs. Baking powder and
baking soda added to the mix are the only things that make it different
from a cake that was baked two hundred years ago. The result is a
moist, very vanilla-y cake that is brilliant with any frosting.

3 cups (300 grams) cake flour, sifted
1 teaspoon baking powder
1 teaspoon baking soda
½ teaspoon kosher salt
1 cup (240 grams) whole milk or
    buttermilk, room temperature

1 tablespoon (13 grams) vanilla
    extract
2 sticks (1 cup; 227 grams) unsalted
    butter, room temperature
2 cups (400 grams) sugar
4 large eggs, room temperature

Preheat the oven to 350°F (180°C). Prepare your pan(s) with Cake
Pan Primer (see page 96) and, depending on the pan(s), line with
parchment paper or cupcake papers.

In a medium bowl, whisk or sift together the cake flour, baking
powder, baking soda, and salt.

In a separate medium bowl or measuring cup, whisk together
the milk and vanilla.

In the bowl of a stand mixer fitted with the paddle attachment
(you can also use a hand mixer and a very large bowl), beat the
butter and sugar on medium speed until much lighter in color
and fluffy, about 4 minutes. Add the eggs, one at a time, beating
on medium speed for 1 minute between each egg. Don't forget
to stop and scrape the sides of the bowl! With the mixer on low
speed, blend in one third of the dry ingredients until the mixture is
streaky. Add half of the vanilla milk mixture, the next third of the

dry ingredients, and the rest of the vanilla milk mixture. Remove the bowl from the mixer and fold in the remaining dry ingredients by hand. Divide the batter evenly between the prepared pan(s), smoothing the tops with an offset spatula.

Bake for the amount of time appropriate for your pan(s) (directions follow) until the top springs back lightly when pressed, the cake starts pulling away from the side of the pan, and a toothpick inserted in the center comes out with just a few crumbs. Transfer to a wire rack and let cool for 10 minutes. Remove from the pan(s), set on wire racks, and let cool completely.

VARIATIONS

Fiori di Sicilia (Flowers of Sicily): Reduce the vanilla extract to 1 teaspoon and add ½ teaspoon lemon extract and ½ teaspoon orange extract.

Citrus: Rub the grated zest of one lemon or one orange into the sugar before creaming with the butter and/or with Lemon or Orange Cake Soak (page 91) or an orange Liquor or Spirit Cake Soak (page 90).

Almond: Reduce the vanilla extract to 1 teaspoon and add 1 teaspoon almond extract.

Coconut: Replace the dairy with an equal amount of full-fat coconut milk. Reduce the vanilla extract to 1 teaspoon and add 1 teaspoon coconut extract and/or brush the cooled layers with Coconut Cake Soak (page 91). Fold 1 cup (50 grams) coconut flakes (sweetened or unsweetened) into the batter before spooning into the pan(s).

Victorian: Reduce the vanilla extract to 2 teaspoons and add ½ teaspoon food-grade rosewater.

Berry: Spread berry jam between the cake layers and/or fill and frost with Berry Swiss Meringue Buttercream (see page 75).

20 TO 25 MINUTES FOR THREE 8-INCH (20 CM) LAYERS

25 TO 30 MINUTES FOR TWO 9-INCH (23 CM) LAYERS

16 TO 18 MINUTES FOR CUPCAKES

25 TO 30 MINUTES FOR A 9 X 13-INCH (23 CM X 33 CM) SHEET CAKE

45 TO 55 MINUTES FOR A BUNDT CAKE

White Sugar Cookies

Makes 48 two-inch (5 cm) cookies

This is the blank canvas of the cookie world, a classic, not-too-sweet, sugary-vanilla dough. Use immediately for drop cookies. If you have time, the recipe can also be used to make slice-and-bake refrigerator cookies, or the dough can be rolled and cut out. However you bake them, the cookies are perfect for decorating with Royal Icing (page 79) or sanding sugars. I'm particularly fond of dunking the tops of the cooled cookies in a thick citrus Confectioners' Sugar Glaze (page 80).

3 cups (375 g) all-purpose flour
1 teaspoon kosher salt
½ teaspoon baking soda
1 cup (200 g) sugar

2 sticks (16 tablespoons;
227 grams) unsalted butter,
room temperature
2 large eggs, room temperature
1 tablespoon vanilla extract

Preheat the oven to 375°F (190°C). Line baking sheets with parchment paper or Sil-Pat mats.

In a medium bowl, whisk together the flour, salt, and baking soda.

In the bowl of a stand mixer fitted with the paddle attachment (you can also use a hand mixer and a large bowl), beat the sugar and butter on medium speed until much lighter in color and well combined, about 3 minutes. Add the eggs, one at a time, beating for 30 seconds after each addition. Don't forget to stop and scrape the sides of the bowl! Beat in the vanilla extract. With the mixer on low speed, mix in the dry ingredients until nearly combined. Stop the mixer and finish mixing by hand until no streaks of flour remain.

For drop cookies: Using a medium (1.5-inch / 4 cm) cookie scoop or a tablespoon, place rounded mounds of dough about 3 inches (8 cm) apart on the prepared baking sheet. Bake for 10 to 12 minutes, until they have spread about 2 inches (5 cm) and are lightly browned on the bottom.

For slice-and-bake: Divide the dough in two pieces and freeze each in a 6-inch long (15 cm) roll (see page 96) for at least 1 hour. When ready to bake, slice off ¼-inch (.6 cm) rounds of the chilled dough, and transfer to the prepared baking sheets. Bake for 12 to 14 minutes, until lightly browned on the bottom.

For rolled cookies: Divide the dough into four equal pieces, wrap in plastic, flatten into thick discs, and refrigerate for at least 2 hours. The dough gets soft quickly, so it's best to roll and cut one disc at a time, leaving the others in the refrigerator. If the dough is too hard to roll, let it sit for 5 minutes and try again. Lightly flour a counter or marble board and, using a rolling pin, turn and roll the dough until you have a large circle that's about ¼-inch (.6 cm) thick. Add a dusting of flour as necessary to keep the dough from sticking, but be careful not to add too much (use no more than ¼ cup [31 grams] extra flour). Cut out your desired shapes and transfer to the prepared baking sheets. Reroll and cut any remaining dough, then remove the next disc from the refrigerator and continue to roll and cut out. Bake for 9 to 12 minutes, until lightly browned on the bottom—check this by lifting one carefully using a metal spatula.

VARIATIONS

Chocolate: Reduce the all-purpose flour to 2¼ cups (281 grams) and add ¾ cup (64 grams) Dutch-processed cocoa powder.

Spice: Add 1 teaspoon cinnamon, 1 teaspoon nutmeg, ½ teaspoon allspice, and ¼ teaspoon cloves to the dry ingredients.

Ginger: Add 2 teaspoons ground ginger to the dry ingredients.

Lemon: Rub the grated zest of one large lemon into the sugar before beating with the butter and/or add 2 teaspoons lemon extract.

Almond: Reduce the vanilla extract to 1 teaspoon and add 2 teaspoons almond extract.

Brown Sugar Cookies

Makes 18 large cookies

The world does not need yet another chocolate chip cookie recipe, but it could use one that can be chocolate chip, or peanut butter, or oatmeal, or mixed fruit, or kitchen sink . . .

2¼ cups (281 grams) all-purpose flour
1 teaspoon kosher salt
1 teaspoon baking soda
1¾ sticks (14 tablespoons; 196 grams) unsalted butter, room temperature

1 cup (220 grams) light brown sugar, packed
½ cup (100 grams) granulated sugar
1 large egg, room temperature
Up to 2 teaspoons any extract
Up to ¾ cup (approx. 170 grams) mix-ins: chocolate chips, nuts, dried fruit

Preheat the oven to 325°F (170°C). Line baking sheets with parchment paper or Sil-Pat mats.

In a medium bowl, whisk together the flour, salt, and baking soda.

In the bowl of a stand mixer fitted with the paddle attachment (you can also use a hand mixer and a large bowl), beat the butter and sugars on medium speed for about 2 minutes. Add the egg and beat for 1 minute. Add the extract and beat until blended. With the mixer running on low speed, add the dry ingredients in three parts, mixing gently until combined. Fold in any mix-ins. Using a 2-inch (5 cm) cookie scoop or a large tablespoon and your fingers, scoop the dough onto the prepared baking sheets, leaving a few inches between each.

Bake, rotating the pans halfway through, until the tops are set and the edges are becoming a deep, lovely caramel color, 18 to 22 minutes. Let cool on the baking sheets for 5 minutes before gently transferring the cookies to a wire rack to cool completely.

Chocolate Chip Cookies: Fold ¾ cup (128 grams) chocolate chips into the dough after the dry ingredients have been incorporated.

Peanut Butter Cookies: Reduce the unsalted butter to ½ cup (1 stick; 114 grams). Add 6 tablespoons (96 grams) peanut butter, creamy or crunchy, and beat it with the butter and sugars.

Oatmeal Cookies: Replace some or all of the flour with old-fashioned oats.

Cherry and White Chocolate Chip Cookies: Fold ⅓ cup (43 grams) dried cherries and ½ cup (85 grams) white chocolate chips into the dough after the dry ingredients have been incorporated.

Coconut Pecan Cookies: Fold ⅓ cup (17 grams) dried coconut (sweetened or unsweetened) and ½ cup (57 grams) toasted chopped pecans into the dough after the dry ingredients have been incorporated.

Basic Quick Bread/Muffins

Makes one 9 × 5-inch (23 cm x 13 cm) loaf, 16 muffins (using a 2-inch [5 cm] cookie scoop), or one 9 × 9-inch (23 cm x 23 cm) cake

This recipe can be adapted countless ways to make a sweet or savory quick bread, muffins, or a simple single-layer cake. There's more breathing room for experimentation here, as you'll see in the variations. What follows is my go-to, but this is one to play around with. Additionally, it requires only two bowls, can be made entirely by hand, and comes together in a snap.

2 cups (250 grams) all-purpose flour or (240 grams) whole-wheat pastry flour
1 teaspoon baking powder
1 teaspoon baking soda
½ teaspoon kosher salt
Up to 1 teaspoon ground spice (optional)
½ to 1 cup (100 to 200 grams) sugar (use less for a more savory loaf or muffins)

2 large eggs, room temperature
1 cup (240 grams) whole milk, room temperature
½ cup (112 grams) neutral oil, such as canola
Up to 1 tablespoon any extract (optional)
Up to ¾ cup (approx. 170 grams) mix-ins such as dried fruit, chocolate, nuts, grated or cubed cheese, or herbs

Preheat the oven to 350°F (180°C). Prepare your pan(s) with Cake Pan Primer (see page 96) and, depending on the pan(s), line with parchment paper or cupcake papers.

In a medium bowl, whisk together the flour, baking powder, baking soda, salt, and ground spice (if using).

In a separate large bowl, whisk together the sugar, eggs, milk, oil, and extract (if using). Fold the dry ingredients into the wet ingredients until just combined (do not overmix). Fold in the mix-ins. Spoon the batter into the prepared pan(s).

Bake for the amount of time appropriate for your pan(s) (directions follow) until the top springs back lightly when pressed, the quick bread or cake starts pulling away from the side of the pan, and a toothpick inserted in the center comes out with just a few crumbs. Transfer to a wire rack and let cool for 10 minutes. Remove from the pan(s), set on a wire rack, and let cool completely.

VARIATIONS

Banana: Use ½ cup (100 grams) sugar. Reduce the dairy (I recommend substituting sour cream for the milk) to ½ cup (120 grams). Add ½ teaspoon ground cinnamon to the dry ingredients and 1 cup (227 grams) pureed very ripe banana to the wet ingredients. If desired, fold in 3 ounces (about 85 grams) toasted walnuts or pecans into the batter before spooning into the pan(s).

Berry Citrus: Rub the grated zest of one large lemon or one medium orange into 1 cup (200 grams) sugar. I recommend substituting yogurt for the milk, though not required. Gently fold 1 cup (about 125 grams) fresh or frozen (not thawed) berries into the batter before spooning into the pan(s). This variation is great topped with Lemon Confectioners' Sugar Glaze (page 80).

Chocolate: Use 1 cup (200 grams) sugar. I recommend substituting sour cream for the milk, though not required. Reduce the flour to 1¼ cups (156 grams) and add ¾ cup (64 grams) cocoa powder. It's a good idea to sift the dry ingredients to break up any lumps of cocoa powder.

Coconut: Use 1 cup (200 grams) sugar. I recommend substituting full-fat coconut milk for the dairy milk and using coconut oil. Use 1 teaspoon coconut extract. Fold in 1 cup (50 grams) dried coconut before spooning the batter into the pan.

Carrot Raisin: Add 2 teaspoons five-spice powder or pumpkin pie spice to the dry ingredients. Fold 1 cup (99 grams) grated carrot and ½ cup (64 grams) raisins into the batter before spooning into the pan.

40 TO 50 MINUTES FOR A 9 × 5-INCH (23 CM X 13 CM) LOAF
20 TO 25 MINUTES FOR MUFFINS
28 TO 35 MINUTES FOR A 9 × 9-INCH (23 CM X 23 CM) CAKE

continues

PB&J: Use 1 cup (200 grams) sugar. Spoon half of the batter into the prepared pan(s). Spread 2 tablespoons peanut butter (if needed, warm for 30 seconds in the microwave to soften) and 2 tablespoons any flavor jam or jelly across the surface of the batter. Spoon the rest of the batter on top.

Pumpkin Chocolate Chip: Use 1 cup (200 grams) sugar. Reduce the milk to ½ cup (120 grams). Add 1 cup (244 grams) pureed pumpkin to the wet ingredients. Fold ½ cup (85 grams) chocolate chips into the batter before spooning into the pan(s).

Cheddar Cheese and Chive: Use ¼ cup (50 grams) sugar. I recommend substituting buttermilk for the milk. Fold 1 cup (228 grams) shredded Cheddar cheese and 2 teaspoons finely chopped fresh chives (use 1 teaspoon if dried) into the batter before spooning into the pan(s).

Ham and Gruyère: Use ¼ cup (50 grams) sugar. I recommend substituting buttermilk for the milk. Fold ½ cup (113 grams) chopped ham and ½ cup (113 grams) shredded or diced Gruyère into the batter before spooning into the pan.

FROSTINGS, FILLINGS, GLAZE, GANACHE, AND MORE

This section could go on forever if I (or my publisher) let it, because there are so many wonderful frostings and filling recipes out there. That said, I've included only those that I find myself using again and again, are versatile, and are relatively simple.

Classic Whipped Cream

Makes about 2 cups (about 454 grams)

One word: cold! Get all of your ingredients—even your bowl and whisk attachment—as cold as possible before you begin. The cool temperature will help you get great lightness and airiness. The simplicity of whipped cream can be such an asset to many baked goods, and its ability to tame the sweet (if you let it) is unmatched. Note, too, that heavy cream and whipping cream are actually the same thing. Different brands refer to the same product with different terms.

A fun trick is to make whipped cream with just a mason jar. Combine the ingredients in a mason jar, cover and close tightly, and shake until whipped. It takes about 5 minutes, so make sure your arm is ready!

1 cup (240 grams) heavy cream or whipping cream, cold

2 tablespoons confectioners' sugar, or to taste (optional)

1 teaspoon vanilla extract, or to taste (optional)

About 15 minutes before beating, place the bowl of a stand mixer and the whisk attachment (or a large bowl and the beaters of a hand mixer) in the refrigerator to chill.

Just before you begin, remove the bowl and attachment (or bowl and beaters) from the refrigerator, and pour the cream into the cold bowl. Beginning on low speed, beat the cream, gradually working up to medium-high speed, and continue to beat until medium to stiff peaks form, 3 to 4 minutes. If using sweetener and/or vanilla, add them to the cream when soft peaks have been reached, after about 2 minutes, and then finish beating.

VARIATION
Chocolate: Once you've reached the soft-peak stage (see page 100), whip in 2 tablespoons cocoa powder, or to taste.

Make-Ahead Whipped Cream

Makes about 2 cups (about 454 grams)

This is the perfect recipe if you need to—or just want to—make a batch of whipped cream in the morning to use that evening or the next day, or if you want to keep a jar of whipped cream in the fridge for a day or two. The addition of sour cream or crème fraîche adds a lovely, mellow tanginess and helps keep any water from seeping out and separating from the refrigerated cream for 24 hours or so.

1 cup (240 grams) heavy cream or whipping cream, cold

2 tablespoons confectioners' sugar, or to taste (optional)

1 teaspoon vanilla extract, or to taste (optional)

4 tablespoons sour cream or crème fraîche

About 15 minutes before beating, place the bowl of a stand mixer and the whisk attachment (or a large bowl and the beaters of a hand mixer) in the refrigerator to chill.

Just before you begin, remove the bowl and attachment (or bowl and beaters) from the refrigerator, and pour the cream into the cold bowl. Beginning on low speed, beat the cream, gradually working up to medium-high speed, and continue to beat until medium to stiff peaks form, 3 to 4 minutes. If using sweetener and/or vanilla extract, add them to the cream when soft peaks have been reached, after about 2 minutes, and then finish beating. Gently whisk in the sour cream or crème fraîche.

Gelatin-Stabilized Whipped Cream

Makes about 2 cups (about 454 grams)

This is one of my obsession recipes; I especially love it for frosting layer cakes. The gelatin lends a pleasing mouthfeel, adds stability (making it ideal for piping), and keeps the whipped cream from separating (the water from the cream) for up to 48 hours. You can adjust the quantity of gelatin and water as needed, using 1 teaspoon gelatin and 4 teaspoons cold water per cup of cream.

1 teaspoon unflavored powdered gelatin

4 teaspoons cold water

1 cup (240 grams) heavy cream

2 tablespoons confectioners' sugar, or to taste (optional)

1 teaspoon vanilla extract, or to taste (optional)

In a small saucepan, whisk together the gelatin and water. Place the pan over low heat and heat the mixture, stirring occasionally, until the gelatin has dissolved, 2 minutes. Let cool for 2 to 3 minutes, but do not let the gelatin set; it needs to be pourable.

In the bowl of a stand mixer fitted with the whisk attachment (you can also use a hand mixer), begin beating the cream on low speed, increasing to medium speed when it has thickened slightly. Add the sweetener and vanilla (if using), increase the speed to medium-high, and continue to beat. When the cream starts to noticeably thicken (you can see lines being left behind the whisk) and with the mixer running, slowly pour the gelatin mixture directly into the whipping cream. Avoid the sides of the bowl, as any gelatin that hits it will solidify against the cold metal. Continue to beat on medium-high speed until the cream has reached medium to stiff peaks, which should take no more than 1 to 2 minutes.

VARIATION

Chocolate: Add 2 tablespoons cocoa powder with the confectioners' sugar and vanilla.

Coconut Whipped Cream

Makes a little more than 1 cup (about 226 grams)

This is the go-to vegan whipped topping. I use Thai Kitchen brand coconut milk, as I've found it to be the most dependable. Plan ahead, as the crucial step for success is chilling the can of coconut milk in the fridge at least 24 hours before beating.

1 can (14 ounces; 400 grams) full-fat coconut milk (preferably Thai Kitchen brand)

2 tablespoons confectioners' sugar, or to taste (optional)
1 teaspoon vanilla extract, or to taste (optional)

Refrigerate the can of coconut milk for at least 24 hours before you plan to make the whipped cream.

Open the can and scoop the firm cream layer on top into the bowl of a stand mixer fitted with the whisk attachment (or a large bowl, if using a hand mixer). Discard the water or use as desired. Beat the cream on medium speed until it is broken up and smooth, about 1 minute. Sift in the sweetener (if using). Beat until light and fluffy, about 2 more minutes. Beat in the extract (if using) on low speed until combined.

VARIATION
Chocolate: Beat in 2 tablespoons cocoa powder with the sweetener.

American-Style Buttercream

Makes about 4 cups (about 905 grams)

Very easy to make, American-Style Buttercream requires no cooking and is a versatile, sweet frosting. This recipe makes enough to generously frost 18 cupcakes or one 9 × 13-inch (23 cm × 33 cm) sheet cake. If you are baking an 8-inch (20 cm) or 9-inch (23 cm) two-layer cake, this amount will fill and frost your cake, but there won't be any left to spare. To be sure you get the coverage you want, I recommend doubling the quantities for layer cakes. Better more than less! You can refrigerate this frosting for up to a week or freeze it for up to three months (just defrost fully before using and whip it up a bit with a mixer to bring it back to life).

3 sticks (1½ cups; 340 grams) unsalted butter, very soft

4 cups (480 grams) confectioners' sugar, sifted

¼ cup (60 grams) heavy cream, cold

¼ teaspoon kosher salt

1 tablespoon vanilla extract (optional)

In the bowl of a stand mixer fitted with the paddle attachment (you can also use a hand mixer and a large bowl), beat the butter on medium speed until increased in volume and lighter in color, about 2 minutes. With the mixer running on low speed, gradually add the sugar, about 1 cup at a time, until all of the sugar has been added and incorporated enough with the butter to stop a great puff from hitting you in the face when you increase the speed. Increase the speed to medium-high and beat for 1 minute. Drizzle in the cream, then add the salt and vanilla extract (if using). Continue beating on medium-high speed until the frosting is light and fluffy, 3 to 5 minutes. Decrease the speed to low and beat for 30 seconds to burst any air bubbles. If the buttercream is too thick, add a little more cream, 1 teaspoon at a time. If it's too thin, add more confectioners' sugar, 1 tablespoon at a time.

VARIATIONS

Chocolate: Replace ½ cup (60 grams) of the confectioners' sugar with ½ cup (43 grams) unsweetened cocoa powder. Sift the cocoa powder and confectioners' sugar well to combine.

Mint: Use 2 teaspoons pure mint extract, or to taste, in place of the vanilla extract.

Citrus: Add 2 teaspoons lemon or orange extract, or to taste, in place of the vanilla extract.

Almond: Reduce the vanilla extract to 1 teaspoon and add 1 teaspoon almond extract, or to taste.

Swiss Meringue Buttercream

Makes 5 cups (about 1,134 grams)

This is my favorite frosting for layer cakes. It is smooth and silky, not too sweet, and pipes nicely. The recipe makes enough to generously frost 18 cupcakes or one 9 × 13-inch (23 cm × 33 cm) sheet cake. I always find that I need (and want) way more Swiss Meringue Buttercream for layer cakes, so, as with the American-Style Buttercream, if you are making an 8-inch (20 cm) or 9-inch (23 cm) cake with two or three layers, I recommend doubling the recipe. It may seem like a lot of frosting, but trust me. Any leftover can be refrigerated for up to a week or frozen for up to three months. Just defrost fully before using and whip it up a bit with a mixer to bring it back to life.

4 large egg whites, gently whisked to break them up

1 cup (200 grams) granulated sugar

3 sticks (1½ cups; 340 grams) unsalted butter, cut into tablespoon-sized pieces, room temperature

1 teaspoon vanilla extract, or to taste

Find a saucepan that's big enough for the bowl you will use in the step to rest on and slightly fit into, without touching the bottom. Fill that saucepan with 2 inches (5 cm) of water and bring to a simmer.

In a heatproof, *very clean* bowl (ideally, that of a stand mixer), gently whisk together the egg whites and sugar. Set the bowl over the simmering water and cook, whisking constantly, until the sugar has dissolved and the mixture is quite warm, about 160°F (71°C), about 5 minutes. Transfer the bowl to a stand mixer fitted with the whisk attachment. Beginning on low speed to avoid splattering, slowly increase the speed to high and beat until you have a stiff-peaked meringue (see page 100) and the bowl is cool to the touch, about 5 minutes.

Switch to the paddle attachment and, with the mixer running on medium-low speed, add the butter a few tablespoons at a time. Once all of the butter has been incorporated, increase the speed to medium-high and beat until it is smooth and fluffy, 3 to 5 minutes. If the frosting separates or appears curdled, just continue to beat on medium-high; it will come back together. If it seems too thin, place the bowl of buttercream in the refrigerator for 10 minutes, then return to the mixer and continue. Once the desired consistency has been reached, reduce the speed to the lowest setting, add the vanilla, and beat to eliminate any trapped air bubbles, about 2 minutes.

VARIATIONS

Chocolate: Fold in 6 ounces (170 grams) melted and cooled chocolate after all of the butter has been incorporated.

Brown Sugar: Replace the 1 cup (200 grams) granulated sugar with an equal amount (1 cup; 220 grams) packed brown sugar, either light or dark.

Mint: Replace the vanilla extract with 2 teaspoons mint extract, or to taste.

Almond: Reduce the vanilla extract to ¼ teaspoon and add 1 teaspoon almond extract, or to taste.

Citrus: Replace the vanilla extract with 1 teaspoon lemon or orange extract, or to taste. Alternatively, fold in 1 cup (about 226 grams) lemon curd.

Berry: Process 1 cup (about 320 grams) berry jam in a food processor until very smooth. Press through a sieve to remove any stray seeds. Fold what remains into the finished buttercream.

Chocolate Ganache

Makes 1½ cups (about 340 grams)

A wunderkind, ganache has many uses. It can be a filling or a frosting or scooped out and eaten as a truffle. Use any type of chocolate, but make sure it's the best you can afford. This recipe can easily be halved or doubled; just keep the chocolate-to-cream ratio equal.

6 ounces (170 grams) best-quality chocolate chips or chunks, bittersweet, milk, or white

1 cup (240 grams) heavy cream

Put the chocolate in a medium heatproof bowl.

In a small saucepan set over low heat, warm the cream until bubbles begin forming around the edges (do not boil), about 3 minutes. Pour the hot cream over the chocolate and let sit for 5 minutes. Gently fold the cream and chocolate together until smooth and glossy. Use immediately as a glaze. To use it as a frosting or filling, let cool to room temperature, then beat with an electric mixer on medium-high speed until fluffy.

Seven-Minute Frosting

Makes about 4 cups (about 907 grams)

Marshmallowy and super-sweet, this is basically Swiss meringue without the buttercream part. I find that this frosting is most delicious with chocolate cakes, as it makes something reminiscent of chocolate cream snack cakes. This recipe makes enough to generously frost 18 cupcakes or one 9 × 13-inch (23 cm × 33 cm) sheet cake. If you are making an 8-inch (20 cm) or 9-inch (23 cm) cake with two or three layers, I recommend doubling the recipe. This does not keep well.

3 large egg whites
1 tablespoon light corn syrup
2 tablespoons water

¾ cup (150 grams) sugar
½ teaspoon vanilla extract, or to taste

Find a saucepan that's big enough for the bowl you will use in the next step to rest on and slightly fit into, without touching the bottom. Fill that saucepan with 2 inches (5 cm) of water and bring to a simmer.

In a heatproof, *very clean* bowl (ideally that of a stand mixer), stir together the egg whites, corn syrup, water, and sugar. Set the bowl over the simmering water and cook, stirring frequently, until the sugar has dissolved and the mixture is quite warm, about 160°F (71°C), about 2 minutes (because of the water and the corn syrup, this will happen faster than with the Swiss Meringue Buttercream).

Transfer the bowl to a stand mixer fitted with the whisk attachment. Beginning on low speed to avoid splattering, slowly increase the speed to high and beat until the frosting is voluminous and shiny, about 5 minutes. Whip in the vanilla extract. Use immediately.

Cream Cheese Frosting

Makes about 6 cups (about 1,360 grams)

I like my cream cheese frosting with a lot less sugar than you find in many recipes out there. For that reason, I up the amount of cream cheese, which I find imparts an extra tang and balance to the frosting. Both the cream cheese and butter must be at warm room temperature (see page 95) when making this icing to ensure a smooth finished product. This recipe makes enough to frost 18 cupcakes or one 9 × 13-inch (23 cm × 33 cm) sheet cake, or to reasonably fill and frost an 8-inch (20 cm) or 9-inch (23 cm) two-layer cake.

16 ounces (2 packages; 450 grams) cream cheese, room temperature
2 sticks (1 cup; 227 grams) unsalted butter, room temperature

2 cups (240 grams) confectioners' sugar, sifted
Pinch of salt
1 teaspoon vanilla extract (optional)

In the bowl of a stand mixer fitted with the paddle attachment (you can also use a hand mixer), beat the cream cheese for about 1 minute to break it up. Add the butter, a few tablespoons at a time, until all of it is mixed in. Add the sugar, salt, and vanilla (if using) and beat on medium-high speed until light and fluffy, about 3 minutes. If you still see small bits of butter, turn the mixer to high and beat for a minute or two, stopping frequently to check if the remaining butter has broken up.

VARIATIONS

Peanut Butter: Reduce the unsalted butter to 1¼ sticks (10 tablespoons; 140 grams). Add ⅔ cup (170 grams) peanut butter, chunky or smooth. It's better to use a processed variety, such as Skippy, versus a natural peanut butter to avoid oil separation.

Chocolate: Sift in ½ cup (43 grams) cocoa powder with the confectioners' sugar.

Royal Icing

Makes about 2 cups (about 454 grams)

Royal icing is the gold standard for cookie decorating. It takes color beautifully, it is relatively inexpensive and easy to make, and the consistency can be easily adjusted (meaning, by using more or less liquid, you can create the lining and flood [or fill] icings used by professional decorators). Air is both a friend and enemy of this icing—it is what causes it to set up and dry, but it can lead to your icing being too dry to use before you've finished decorating. That said, until you're ready to let it dry, keep your bowl(s) covered with a wet paper towel as you're using the icing.

1 pound (454 grams) confectioners' sugar

2 large egg whites or 5 tablespoons (75 grams) meringue powder

½ cup (120 grams) water (if using meringue powder; more or less as needed to reach desired consistency)

In a medium bowl, combine the sugar and egg whites or meringue powder. If using the meringue powder, slowly stir in the water, a tablespoon at a time, until the desired consistency is reached. The frosting is now ready for general use. If not using immediately, refrigerate for up to a week in the most airtight container you have.

For lining icing—which is a bit thinner and good for outlining a cookie or a design—you want a soft peak to form when a spoon is lifted from the icing (see page 100). Add more water if needed.

For flood icing—which is very loose and used to fill or flood in a design on a cookie—add more water, a little at a time, until you reach a consistency similar to that of maple syrup. When a spoon is lifted from the bowl, the icing should ribbon down, disappearing in 6 to 8 seconds.

Basic Confectioners' Sugar Glaze

Makes ½ cup (about 113 grams)

This basic glaze can be used on anything from loaf cakes, muffins, and cupcakes to Bundt cakes—and it can even be drizzled atop a layer cake. Start with less liquid and add more as needed to reach the desired consistency; the recipe can easily be doubled, tripled . . .

1½ cups (150 grams) confectioners' sugar, sifted
1 to 4 tablespoons liquid as needed, such as water, milk, cream, liqueur, or citrus juice

1 teaspoon vanilla extract (optional)

In a medium bowl, whisk together the sugar and liquid until smooth. Add the vanilla (if using). If it's too thick, add more liquid.

VARIATIONS

Mint: Use milk or water for the liquid. Replace the vanilla extract with ½ teaspoon mint extract, or to taste.

Orange: Use orange juice and/or orange-flavored liqueur for the liquid, and/or replace the vanilla extract with 1 teaspoon orange extract.

Lemon: Use fresh lemon juice for the liquid, and/or replace the vanilla extract with 1 teaspoon lemon extract.

Basic Caramel Sauce

Makes 1¼ cups (about 284 grams)

Caramel sauce is delicious over just about anything, but I find it's especially delicious spread between cake layers or spooned on top of cupcakes before frosting. Adding a bit of salt takes it up a notch (see Variation).

1 cup (200 grams) sugar
¼ cup (63 grams) water
2 tablespoons light corn syrup

½ cup (120 grams) heavy cream, room temperature
1 teaspoon vanilla extract

In a medium, heavy-bottomed, light-colored (white or silver, so that you can really watch the color change) saucepan, gently combine the sugar, water, and corn syrup. Do your best not to let sugar granules splash up the sides of the pan. If you do, use a wet pastry brush to wipe them down. Set the pan over medium heat—do not stir! You can gently agitate the pan if you're anxious, but it's best to let it be. Either clip a candy thermometer to the side of the pan and let cook until it reaches 350°F (180°C) or use your nose and your eyes: the smell of caramel will fill the air and the sugar in the pot will quickly turn from a light gold to a copper penny color. Immediately remove the pan from the heat. Slowly whisk in the cream; be careful, as the caramel will pop and bubble. Whisk in the vanilla. Let cool.

VARIATION
Salted Caramel Sauce: Whisk 1 teaspoon (or to taste) fine sea salt or kosher salt into the sauce after the vanilla, but before the sauce has cooled.

Browned Butter

Makes 4 ounces (113 grams)

Use this deeply flavored, nutty butter in any recipe that calls for melted butter.

1 stick (1 cup; 227 grams) butter
  (unsalted or salted, your choice)

In a light-colored (white or silver, so that you can really watch the color change) saucepan set over medium heat, melt the butter. There is no need to stir the butter as it melts, but keep a close eye on it. Once you hear popping (the water cooking away), gently swirl the pan, then set it back on the stove, turning the heat to medium-low. Here's where you want to watch it like a hawk. You will start to see brown bits at the bottom of the pan. Using a heatproof spatula, stir gently to keep everything incorporated and melting evenly. After about 7 minutes, watch for the melted butter to turn a lovely medium gold shade, like perfectly done toast. Immediately remove the pan from the heat (it will continue to brown a bit more after removing from the heat). Stir with the spatula and let cool before using.

Crumb Topping

Makes about 2 cups (about 400 grams)

This all-purpose crumb topping can be used on cakes, muffins, crumbles, or pies. I sometimes use whole-wheat flour instead of all-purpose flour for a nuttier taste. This recipe doubles well (and that's always a good idea).

1½ cups (188 grams) all-purpose flour
1¼ cups (263 grams) light brown sugar, packed
2 teaspoons ground cinnamon
¾ teaspoon kosher salt
1½ sticks (12 tablespoons; 170 grams) unsalted butter, cold and diced into small pieces

In a medium bowl, whisk together the flour, sugar, cinnamon, and salt. Using your fingers, work the cold butter into the flour mixture until you've achieved a range of clump sizes, from large to small.

Scatter on top of your batter or baking dish of fruit and bake as indicated (usually at 350°F [180°C] until golden and fragrant, but make sure to follow instructions specific to your baked good).

You can also spread out the clumps in a single layer on a Sil-Pat or parchment-lined baking sheet and bake at 350° (180°C) until fragrant and golden brown, 15 to 18 minutes, stirring once with a fork after 10 minutes to break up any crumbs that have melted together. Let cool completely. These are delicious layered with whipped cream and pudding or mousse, stirred into yogurt, or sprinkled on top of ice cream or fruit.

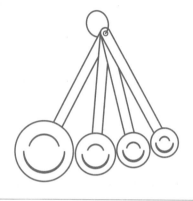

SUBSTITUTIONS

CAKE FLOUR (1 CUP)

1 cup minus 2 tablespoons (109 grams) all-purpose flour plus
2 tablespoons cornstarch

SIFTED ALL-PURPOSE OR CAKE FLOUR (1 CUP)

1 cup minus 2 tablespoons (109 grams for all-purpose flour;
88 grams for cake flour)

SELF-RISING FLOUR (1 CUP)

1 cup (125 grams) all-purpose flour plus 1½ teaspoons baking
powder and ⅛ teaspoon salt

BROWN SUGAR (1 CUP)

FOR LIGHT BROWN: 1 cup (200 grams) granulated sugar
plus 1½ tablespoons molasses

FOR DARK BROWN: 1 cup (200 grams) granulated sugar
plus ¼ cup (85 grams) molasses

IF YOU HAVE ONLY LIGHT BROWN BUT NEED DARK BROWN:
1 cup (220 grams) light brown sugar plus 1 tablespoon molasses

IF YOU HAVE ONLY DARK BROWN BUT NEED LIGHT BROWN:
½ cup (100 grams) granulated sugar plus 1 cup (220 grams)
dark brown sugar. Measure your light brown sugar out of that
mixture.

CASTOR OR SUPERFINE SUGAR

Process granulated (regular white) sugar in a food processor until, well, superfine.

BAKING POWDER (1 TEASPOON)

¼ teaspoon baking soda plus ½ teaspoon cream of tartar

BUTTERMILK (1 CUP)

1 tablespoon white vinegar or lemon juice plus enough milk to make 1 cup (about 225 grams)

CRÈME FRAÎCHE (1 CUP)

½ cup (120 grams) each sour cream and heavy cream

CONFECTIONERS' (POWDERED) SUGAR (1 CUP)

Process 1 cup (200 grams) granulated sugar and 1 tablespoon cornstarch in a food processor until powdery.

EGG (1 LARGE EGG)

2½ tablespoons flax meal plus 3 tablespoons water,
or ½ banana, or 1 tablespoon applesauce

The American Egg Board gives the following chart on their immensely helpful website, incredibleegg.org. The column on the left indicates the number of large eggs called for in a recipe, while the proceeding numbers to the right indicate how many of each particular size you can substitute instead of large.

L	J	XL	M
1	1	1	1
2	2	2	2
3	2	3	3
4	3	4	5
5	4	4	6
6	5	5	7

DIY

EXTRACTS

For all of these extracts, store in a cool, dark place and shake the container every few days until the flavors have fully developed. Citrus extracts develop the quickest—usually after a few weeks. Give the mint a month or so, then strain out the leaves when the desired strength is reached. I find that vanilla can take up to six months to get good and strong.

VANILLA: Per 1 cup (240 grams) vodka, add 3 beans

CITRUS: Per 1 cup (240 grams) vodka, use the grated zest of
4 oranges, 5 lemons or limes, or 3 grapefruit

MINT: Per 1 cup (240 grams) vodka, muddle ½ cup
(about 15 grams) fresh mint leaves into the vodka

VANILLA BEAN PASTE

In a food processor, process 3 fat, fresh vanilla beans until they are well broken up. Transfer to a small bowl and stir in 2 teaspoons vanilla extract and ¼ cup (85 grams) agave nectar or vegetable glycerin. Press through a fine mesh strainer to remove pulpy bits. Store in an airtight container in a cool, dark place (like a kitchen cupboard) for up to two months.

FLAVORED SUGARS

VANILLA: Pour 1 cup (100 grams) granulated sugar into a small
bowl. Add 3 fresh or dried vanilla beans that have been roughly

chopped. Stir and put into an airtight jar. Let sit in a cool, dark place for a few weeks, shaking on occasion. To replenish, you can top off the sugar you've used in the original jar, and replace the vanilla beans every year or so.

LAVENDER, THYME, ROSEMARY, AND SO ON: Start with 1 teaspoon dried herb per cup of sugar and work your way stronger. Let sit in a cool, dark place for a few weeks, shaking on occasion.

FRUIT SUGARS: Using a food processor, mortar and pestle, or just your hands, pulverize ½ cup of any freeze-dried fruit. Thoroughly blend it with 1 cup (200 grams) granulated sugar in a small bowl. The sugar is ready to use immediately.

SIMPLE SYRUP

Combine 1 cup (240 grams) water and 1 cup (200 grams) sugar (plain or flavored, page 89) in a small saucepan. Bring to a boil, reduce the heat to low, and simmer until all of the sugar has dissolved, about 3 minutes. Remove the pan from the heat. Let cool completely. Store in an airtight container in the refrigerator for up to six months.

For ideas on flavoring simple syrup, see the Cake Soaks (next section), since that's essentially what they are.

CAKE SOAKS

When you want extra-moist cake, or if you want to add a boost of flavor to cake, try using a cake soak. Simple syrup alone works brilliantly to help moisten layers, and flavoring the syrup is a cinch. Here are some of my favorite flavored variations:

MINT: Add 2 teaspoons pure mint extract to the cooled simple syrup.

LIQUOR OR SPIRIT: Add ¼ cup (48 grams) orange liqueur (such as Cointreau or Grand Marnier) or ¼ cup (48 grams) spirit (such as bourbon, whiskey, or rum) to the cooled simple syrup.

COCONUT: Add 4 teaspoons coconut extract to the cooled simple syrup.

LAVENDER: Toss 2 tablespoons dried lavender with the sugar before mixing with the water and bringing to boil on the stove top. Strain out the flowers before using or storing.

LEMON OR ORANGE: Add 2 tablespoons lemon or orange extract to the cooled simple syrup.

NATURAL FOOD COLORING

You can get bold, bright colors using all-natural foods, and often the tones are a bit earthier, which is pleasing. Start with just a few drops or shakes at a time to build color gradually. Note that some of these will affect the taste of your finished product.

RED: Pomegranate juice

ORANGE: Carrot juice or paprika

YELLOW: Ground turmeric or saffron (use both of these very sparingly)

GREEN: Fresh spinach juice or matcha tea powder

BLUE: Add a pinch of baking soda to red cabbage juice*

PURPLE: Red cabbage juice*

PINK: Beet juice

BROWN: Instant coffee or espresso powder, or strong black tea

*To make red cabbage juice, put ¼ head fresh red cabbage into a pot. Add water to cover. Bring to a boil, reduce the heat to low, and simmer for 15 minutes. Strain, discarding the solids, and let the juice cool.

COLORED SUGARS

Put ½ cup (100 grams) granulated sugar into a glass or metal bowl. A few drops at a time, add gel paste or water-based food coloring, blending well, until the desired color is reached. Spread the colored sugar onto a rimmed baking sheet in a thin layer. Let dry for 20 minutes. Store indefinitely in an airtight container.

EDIBLE GLITTER

Preheat the oven to 275°F (140°C). In a small bowl, thoroughly mix together ½ teaspoon gum arabic, ½ teaspoon hot water, and ½ teaspoon luster dust in the metallic color of your choice. Spread the mixture onto a nonstick baking mat set on a cookie sheet in a thin layer; the mixture will separate and cluster together, which is fine. Bake for 10 minutes, or until the strands and blobs of color pull easily from the baking sheet. Let cool completely, then rub through a mesh sifter; the size of holes in the mesh will determine the size of your glitter.

SPRINKLES

Tint a batch of Royal Icing (page 79) to your desired color. Thin the icing slightly so that it is at the "fill" consistency (see page 79). Using a pastry bag fitted with a #2 round tip, or a parchment paper piping bag (see page 99) with the smallest cut tip possible, pipe the icing in long rows onto sheets of wax paper. Let dry overnight. Using a sharp knife, cut or chop the rows into the desired size.

HOW-TO

BE A MACGYVER BAKER

The time may come when you find yourself without the proper supplies necessary to decorate, finish, or serve baked goods. In those instances, channel your inner MacGyver and get creative.

- Prick tons of holes in the bottom of a paper cup with a pushpin to make a sifter for confectioners' sugar.

- Use coffee filters as plates *and* napkins (my friend Lynn dubbed this the "plapkin").

- To make an easy cake topper, grab a wooden coffee stirrer and tape or glue on an image cut from a printout or magazine.

- In a pinch, a long strand of dental floss (ideally unflavored) can be used to cleanly cut a cake.

- Set up a temporary cake stand with an upturned, sturdy tumbler and a dinner plate.

DECORATE WITH UNEXPECTED TOOLS

A few everyday items come in quite handy with certain decorating tasks:

- Tweezers are small and precise enough to use for moving miniatures or sprinkles around.

- An X-Acto knife and scissors are necessary for cutting out stencils for cake or cupcake toppers.

- Toothpicks and bamboo skewers are perfect for cake or cupcake toppers. Use tape or nontoxic glue to attach the images for the toppers to the toothpicks or skewers; you can cut down the length of the skewers as needed with scissors.

- Washi tape is great for making quick flag toppers; fold a piece together over the end of a toothpick or bamboo skewer. You can also use scissors to cut out an inverse triangle, making a swallow-tailed flag.

TEST THE ACCURACY OF A DIGITAL SCALE
The shiniest, newest nickel you have should weigh 5 grams.

BRING EGGS TO ROOM TEMPERATURE IN A HURRY
Put whole eggs, still in their shells, in a bowl and fill with warm (not hot!) water to cover. Let sit 5 minutes.

KNOW WHEN BUTTER IS AT ROOM TEMPERATURE
Butter has reached the "room temperature" stage when it is between 65°F and 67°F (18°C and 19°C). When pressed, there will be some give, but your finger won't press right through; the butter will keep its shape. If in stick form, the butter should be able to softly bend without breaking or cracking. If a recipe calls for "cool room temperature," aim for 63°F (17°C) and butter that holds just a slight press of a finger. Conversely, "warm room temperature" butter will depress a bit farther and register closer to 68°F (20°C).

SOFTEN BUTTER IN A HURRY
If frozen: Use a standard box grater to shred the butter into small pieces.

If just out of the fridge: Cut the butter into small pieces and spread out in a single layer on a sheet of wax paper. Let sit at room temperature for 5 minutes. Alternatively, smash between sheets of wax paper with a rolling pin.

PREPARE COOKIE DOUGH FOR PERFECTLY ROUND COOKIES

For slice-and-bake refrigerator cookies, roll the dough into a log, wrap with plastic or parchment paper, and fit the log into an empty paper towel tube that's been cut open lengthwise. Refrigerate or freeze until ready to cut and bake.

For drop cookies, using a small ice cream scoop, evenly portion out the dough, scraping any excess off the cookie ball on the edge of the bowl before dropping the dough onto a baking sheet. Place the baking sheet with the scooped cookies into the freezer for a few hours or overnight, then transfer the cookies to a freezer-safe storage bag or container.

PREPARE CAKE PANS

There are many methods, but my favorite uses what I call Cake Pan Primer. In a large bowl, thoroughly whisk together ½ cup (112 grams) neutral oil (canola and grapeseed work well), ½ cup (112 grams) vegetable shortening, and ½ cup (63 grams) all-purpose or gluten-free flour until the mixture forms a smooth paste. You will have about 9 ounces (255 grams) of primer. Refrigerate in an airtight container for up to six months. To grease cake pans with it, use a pastry brush or silicone basting brush to paint the primer into every little nook and cranny of the pan(s). If using layer cake or sheet cake pans, use a standard parchment liner on top of the coating of primer, and then paint a little primer on the parchment as well.

CUT A LAYER CAKE

This is the basic way to cut eight slices from a round layer cake, all at one time, as well as a way to maximize the number of slices you can get from a standard round cake. I find that it's helpful to have a damp cloth nearby to wipe excess frosting from the knife blade between cuts.

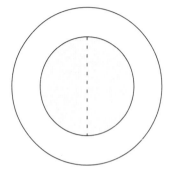

Using a clean, sharp knife, cut straight through the middle of the cake from edge to edge.

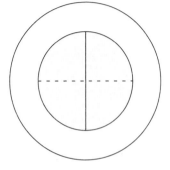

Rotate 45 degrees and repeat the edge-to-edge cut.

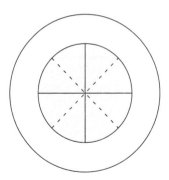

Rotate again, and slice through two of the pieces. Repeat.

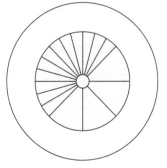

If you need to feed a large number, first cut a circle in the center of the cake, then cut slices all along the cake at whatever thickness is desired.

CUT A PARCHMENT PAPER CIRCLE TO LINE A PAN

You can find pre-cut parchment paper circles for the most common cake pan sizes at specialty baking or craft stores, or online (look for brands like Regency and Wilton), but it's still good to know how to cut your own circles to size from parchment you have in your pantry.

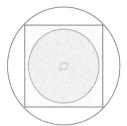

Tear off a sheet of parchment paper slightly larger than your pan.

Fold the sheet of parchment in half lengthwise, then in half again widthwise.

Repeat the same fold.

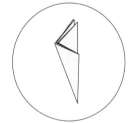

With the creased edges on the bottom and right sides, fold the bottom crease to meet the right side creased edge.

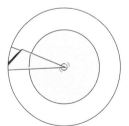

Place the tip of the triangle at the midpoint on the bottom of the pan. Mark where the base of the triangle meets the edge of the pan.

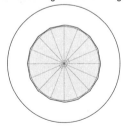

Cut through the mark and unfold the paper.

MAKE A PARCHMENT PAPER PIPING BAG, AKA PAPER CORNET

A piping bag is an essential tool for decorating cakes and cookies, and you can easily make one (or many) from a roll of parchment paper.

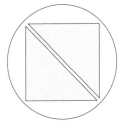

Tear off a 12-inch-long (30 cm) sheet of parchment paper and fold in half, forming two triangles. Cut through the crease, leaving two triangles.

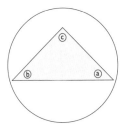

Lay one of the triangles in front of you, long edge closest, with the point at the top. Label the bottom right corner A, the bottom left corner B, and the peak C.

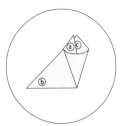

Fold corner A toward corner C, firmly twisting the paper into a cone shape.

Grab corner B and pull it around from front to back.

Join all three points together and tightly fold down.

Fill with frosting or batter, and then cut off the tip as desired, keeping in mind the smaller the cut = the smaller the hole = the finer the line.

CUT VARIOUS DECORATING TIPS ON A PAPER CORNET

Petals and leaves

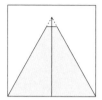

Lines, writing, and dots

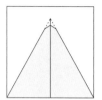

Roses

Ribbons

TELL WHICH PEAK YOU'VE REACHED

Soft peak: will not hold
its shape; any peaks will
immediately collapse

Medium or firm peak:
holds its shape, but the tip
will curl over

Stiff peak: holds a firm
point, even if turned
upside down

STORE WHOLE EGGS, EGG WHITES

NOTE: Egg yolks cannot be frozen without adulteration, which is why I haven't included the instructions for doing so.

Beat each egg or egg white until thoroughly blended. Pour into a freezer-safe container, mark how many it contains, and freeze for up to six months. You can also use ice cube trays to freeze whole eggs or whites separately. Once they are frozen, remove from the tray and put in a freezer-safe storage bag or container. Store for up to six months. Let thaw completely before using.

DECORATING

There's no need for fondant, impeccable piping skills, or a Pinterest-worthy prop room full of supplies to decorate baked goods with charm, style, and wit. Try the following on your cakes, cookies, or cupcakes.

CARAMEL SAUCE AND CHOCOLATE GANACHE

It never ceases to amaze me how impressive it looks when you liberally pour caramel sauce or chocolate ganache all over the top of a cake, and then leave it to drip dramatically down the sides. See page 81 for Basic Caramel Sauce and page 76 for Chocolate Ganache.

COLOR

Going beyond the bottles of color sold in grocery stores can be intimidating, but with a little knowledge, it is quite simple to create really beautiful, colorful edibles. Food color comes in many forms and formulas, from paste to powder, spray paint to marker. Following is a list of the four basic types of food color and the uses for which they are best employed.

GEL PASTE COLOR: This all-purpose colorant is what professionals (and passionate amateurs) use for coloring buttercreams and frostings, cake and cookie batters, or tinting bread dough. The color is very concentrated—a little goes a long way—so start with just the tiniest dab. Of note when using for buttercream: gel colors intensify when exposed to cold (like overnight in the refrigerator). To achieve and maintain your desired color, begin by tinting 1 cup (227 grams) buttercream close to the color you hope to obtain, then microwave on high power for 30 seconds. The result will represent the most intense color. Use that to tint your buttercream or gauge how much color to add.

OIL-BASED COLOR: Sometimes called "candy color," this type of coloring is used for white chocolate.

POWDER COLOR: This is my other favorite (along with gel paste), because the colors are super concentrated and versatile. I especially love powdered metallics. Use alone as a color dust, or mix it with a few drops of vodka or lemon juice to make edible paint.

WATER-BASED COLOR: This is the type most commonly found at the grocery store. Use it for tinting buttercream frosting as well as batters and doughs. There is an ingenious color formula chart online for creating dozens of different colors using just the standard red, yellow, blue, and green that come in the box; search "frost by the numbers" at foodnetwork.com. You can also draw directly onto frosted cakes and iced cookies with edible markers. Note that because of the water base, the color may bleed.

If you aren't a fan of industrial color—or are just curious to try coloring like what your great-grandmother would have used—see page 91 for a list of natural food colorants.

ICING SHEETS

You can print your own edible icing sheets at home using a special printer that uses edible ink and edible icing sheets. Also, many online companies will print your own design for you, and pre-made designs are available. (See Resources, page 106.)

FLOWERS

One of the easiest and most cost-effective ways to add oomph to a cake is to top it with flowers and/or greenery. For safety reasons, if you choose fresh materials, use those grown organically and, when in doubt, search the plant at poison.org to check for toxicity. Otherwise, the fake flowers available these days from craft shops can be just as good. You can also find pre-made sugar paste flowers in most baking supply shops or online. (See Resources, page 106.)

DOLLHOUSE AND RAILROAD MINIATURES

Tiny things = instant charm. An amazing variety of miniatures is available these days at craft and hobby stores and online. Try searching online for "railroad miniatures" and "dollhouse miniatures." Create a winter wonderland with tiny trees set on top of a white-frosted or coconut layer cake, make a village scene using little houses and buildings, put miniature ice-skating figures on top of an ice-blue cake, or a few figures in swimming gear on top of an ocean-blue cake. The possibilities are endless.

FREEZE-DRIED FRUITS AND VEGETABLES

Add bright flavor, concentrated color, and great texture to any baked good by adding freeze-dried fruits and vegetables. I tend to like berries best, but any freeze-dried item will work. Keep them whole, if you like, or crush them with your hands or a rolling pin to make a more dustlike sprinkle.

MOLDS FOR CANDY AND CHOCOLATE

Baking supply shops and online retailers sell ready-made molds that you can use to make candy or chocolate accents. There are also food-grade molding kits that let you make a mold from just about anything. (See Resources, page 106.)

PAPER CUTOUTS

If you can cut it out, it can be put on a cake. If you want to lay a cutout directly onto the surface, use nontoxic glue to attach parchment paper to the back of the image before cutting it out. To make a cake or cupcake topper, tape or glue the cutout to a toothpick or bamboo skewer trimmed to size.

ROYAL ICING

Two words: Patti Paige, the woman behind bakedideas.com. She creates some of the most beautiful, interesting iced cookies around. Take a look at her website or, better yet, pick up a copy of her book, *You Can't Judge a Cookie by Its Cutter*, to learn how to using royal icing like Rembrandt used oil paints. (See page 79 for the Royal Icing recipe.)

STENCILS

I love using stencils of all kinds to decorate layer cakes. There are plenty of pre-cut ones available, and one of my favorite sources is evilcakegenius.com. It's also worth looking in the stencils section at hardware or craft stores—even if they're meant for painting walls or furniture, they still work well on cake! You can easily make your own by printing out words or images on standard paper or card stock and cutting out with a craft knife or scissors the areas you want to fill with color or texture. Just don't press the stencil too hard onto the cake top; I recommend stenciling on a cold cake, as it's easier to avoid messing up the icing. Beyond paper and pre-cut, you can use just about any material: lace, a doily, or a gridded cooling rack, to name a few. Ingredients such as cocoa powder and confectioners' sugar adhere well on their own, but if you want to use looser materials like sprinkles, edible glitter, or colored sugars, I recommend lightly painting the area to be filled in with corn syrup or vegetable glycerin before application to ensure that the little bits and baubles stay put. See page 92 for how to make your own sprinkles, edible glitter, and colored sugars.

RESOURCES

PRINT

All Cakes Considered by Melissa Gray

Amy's Bread and *The Sweeter Side of Amy's Bread* by Amy Scherber and Toy Kim Dupree

BabyCakes, BabyCakes Covers the Classics, and *Bread & Butter* by Erin McKenna

Baked, Baked Explorations, Baked Elements, and *Baked Occasions* by Matt Lewis and Renato Poliafito

BakeWise by Shirley O. Corriher

The Baking Answer Book by Lauren Chattman

Baking from My Home to Yours, Baking Chez Moi, and *Baking with Julia* by Dorrie Greenspan

Baking Illustrated by the editors of *Cook's Illustrated* magazine

Baking in America by Greg Patent

Baking with Less Sugar, Flour, and *Flour, Too* by Joanne Chang

Bundt Cake Bliss by Susanna Short

The Cake Bible, The Baking Bible, and *The Bread Bible* by Rose Levy Beranbaum

Crumb by Ruby Tandoh

The Fannie Farmer Baking Book by Marion Cunningham

Flavor Flours by Alice Medrich

Flourless by Nicole Spiridakis

Flour Water Salt Yeast by Ken Forkish

Food52 Baking by the editors of Food52

The Four & Twenty Blackbirds Pie Book by Emily Elsen
and Melissa Elsen

Good to the Grain by Kim Boyce

Grandbaby Cakes by Jocelyn Delk Adams

Home Baked by Yvette van Boven

The Hot Bread Kitchen Cookbook by Jesamyn Waldman Rodriguez

How Baking Works by Paula I. Figoni

How to Be a Domestic Goddess by Nigella Lawson

Ice Box Cakes by Jean Sagendorph and Jessie Sheehan

Joy the Baker Cookbook and *Homemade Decadence* by Joy Wilson

The King Arthur Flour Baker's Companion by King Arthur Flour

The Kitchn Cookbook by Sara Kate Gillingham and Faith Durand

Maida Heatter's Cakes and *Maida Heatter's Cookies* by Maida Heatter

Martha Stewart's Baking Handbook, *Martha Stewart's Cakes*,
Martha Stewart's Cookies, and *Martha Stewart's Pies and Tarts*
by Martha Stewart

Modern Art Desserts by Caitlin Freeman

The Modern Baker, *Perfect Cakes*, *Bake!*, *Nick Malgieri's Pastry*, and
Nick Malgieri's Bread by Nick Malgieri

Momofuku Milk Bar by Christina Tosi

My Bread by Jim Lahey

One Bowl Baking by Yvonne Ruperti

Ovenly by Agatha Kulaga and Erin Patinkin

Pie in the Sky by Susan G. Purdy

Quinntessential Baking by Francis Quinn

Ready for Dessert by David Lebovitz

Real Sweet and *Real Vanilla* by Shauna Server

The Secret Lives of Baked Goods by Jessie Oleson Moore

The Simple Art of Perfect Baking by Flo Braker

Tartine Bread by Chad Robertson

Vegan Cupcakes Take Over the World, Vegan Cookies Invade Your Cookie Jar, and *Vegan Pie in the Sky* by Isa Chandra Moskowitz

Vintage Cakes by Julie Richardson

The Violet Bakery Cookbook by Claire Ptak

Whole-Grain Mornings by Megan Gordon

You Can't Judge a Cookie by Its Cutter by Patti Paige

A FEW FAVORITE BAKING BLOGS AND WEBSITES

Allrecipes
allrecipes.com

Apt. 2B Baking Co.
apt2bbakingco.com

Cafe Fernando
cafefernando.com

Cook's Illustrated
cooksillustrated.com

David Lebovitz
davidlebovitz.com

Food 52
food52.com

Jessie Sheehan Bakes
jessiesheehanbakes.com

Joy of Baking
joyofbaking.com

Joy the Baker
joythebaker.com

King Arthur Flour
kingarthurflour.com

The Kitchn
thekitchn.com

Lottie + Doof
lottieanddoof.com

Martha Stewart
marthastewart.com

Pastry Scoop
pastryscoop.com

Smitten Kitchen
smittenkitchen.com

Sweetapolita
sweetapolita.com

A Sweet Spoonful
asweetspoonful.com

Traditional Oven
traditionaloven.com

ONLINE BAKING AND DECORATING CLASSES

Craftsy
craftsy.com

Creativebug
creativebug.com

BAKING AND DECORATING SUPPLIES

Amazon
amazon.com

King Arthur Flour
kingarthurflour.com

The Baker's Kitchen
thebakerskitchen.net

Kitchen Krafts
kitchenkrafts.com

Color Garden
colorgarden.net

Michaels
michaels.com

Doll House Supplies
dollhousesupplies.com

The Mouse Market
themousemarket.com

Etsy
etsy.com

NY Cake
nycake.com

Evil Cake Genius
evilcakegenius.com

Pastry Chef Central
pastrychef.com

Fancy Flours
fancyflours.com

Sur la Table
surlatable.com

Hobby Linc
hobbylinc.com

Williams-Sonoma
williams-sonoma.com

JB Prince
jbprince.com

Wilton
wilton.com

THANK YOU

To Bea and Evan. I'm glad I get to spend the rest of my life appreciating you both, because this one page sure isn't going to cut it.

To Mom and Paul, Dad and Moss. Ditto. I mean, seriously, how do I even begin?

To Katie, Jen, Jenny, Kiss, Whit, Debbie, Christy, Lisa, and the rest of my beautiful, weird, wonderful family, near and far.

To Ben Gibson and Pop Chart Labs for bringing the book to life.

To my work family at Penguin, who has cheered me on and faithfully eaten everything I've brought in for years and years, even when it kinda sucked.

To my stalwart gang of recipe testers, Jessie, Stephanie W., Caitlin, Julia, Farin, Rebecca, Stephanie B., and Linda.

To Julia and Grace for being so incredibly kind and lovely.

To Renato and Matt for starting it all with your Dreamy Coconut Cake.

To Bonnie Slotnick for a home away from home, Laura Shapiro for her inspiration, and George Pitts for being part of the beginning.

To Candice, Michael, Kate, and Meg for a lifetime; to Russell for leaving the kitchen alone; and to all of my friends for their support, kind words, and alcoholic beverages.

To Amanda Hesser, Merrill Stubbs, and everyone at Food52 for being in since day one.

To the lovely people at Archestratus, Dry Goods Brooklyn, Willoughby General, Mondays Whole Foods, and Annie's Blue Ribbon General Store for falling in love with the baker's twine loop as much as I did.

And last, but certainly not least, to Kari Stuart, Ashley Meyer, Marysarah Quinn, and the whole lot at Clarkson Potter for making my dream come true.

RECIPE LIST